First
Facts

Community Helpers at Work

# A Day in the Life of a
# Dentist

by Heather Adamson

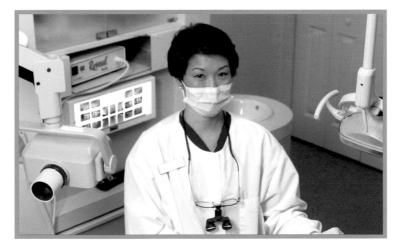

**Consultant:**
Karen M. Yoder, Ph.D.
Director, Division of Community Dentistry
Indiana University School of Dentistry

Capstone
press
Mankato, Minnesota

First Facts is published by Capstone Press
151 Good Counsel Drive, P.O. Box 669, Mankato, Minnesota 56002
http://www.capstone-press.com

*Library of Congress Cataloging-in-Publication Data*
Adamson, Heather, 1974–
  A day in the life of a dentist / by Heather Adamson.
    p. cm.— (First facts. Community helpers at work)
  Includes bibliographical references and index.
  Contents: How do dentists start their days?—What do dentists wear?—Who helps
    dentists?—What do dentists eat for lunch?—What happens during a checkup?—What
    happens in a dentist's lab?—What tools do dentists use?—Why do people need to visit
    the dentist?—Equipment photo diagram.
  ISBN 0-7368-2282-8 (hardcover)
  1. Dentistry—Juvenile literature. [1. Dentistry. 2. Dentists. 3. Occupations.] I. Title. II.
    Series.
RK63.A33 2004
617.6—dc21                                                                    2003000153

**Credits**
Jennifer Schonborn, series and book designer; Jim Foell, photographer; Eric Kudalis,
    product planning editor

**Artistic Effects**
Comstock, Eyewire, Ingram Publishing, PhotoDisc Inc.

Capstone Press thanks Dr. Theresa Fong for her cooperation in making this book. Thanks
also to Dr. Keith Flack and the staff of North Mankato Family Dentistry for their help in
photographing this book.

1 2 3 4 5 6 08 07 06 05 04 03

# Table of Contents

How do dentists start their days? . . . . . . . . . . . . . .4

What do dentists wear? . . . . . . . . . . . . . . . . . . . . . . .7

Who helps dentists? . . . . . . . . . . . . . . . . . . . . . . . .8

What do dentists eat for lunch? . . . . . . . . . . . . . .11

What happens at a checkup? . . . . . . . . . . . . . . . .12

What happens in a dentist's lab? . . . . . . . . . . . . .14

What tools do dentists use? . . . . . . . . . . . . . . . .16

Why do people need to
visit the dentist? . . . . . . . . . . . . . . . . . . . . . . . . .18

Amazing But True! . . . . . . . . . . . . . . . . . . . . . . . .20

Equipment Photo Diagram . . . . . . . . . . . . . . . . .20

Glossary . . . . . . . . . . . . . . . . . . . . . . . . . . . . . . . .22

Read More . . . . . . . . . . . . . . . . . . . . . . . . . . . . . .23

Internet Sites . . . . . . . . . . . . . . . . . . . . . . . . . . . .23

Index . . . . . . . . . . . . . . . . . . . . . . . . . . . . . . . . . .24

# How do dentists start their days?

Each morning, dentists get the office ready for patients. Dr. Fong plans the day with the office workers. They check if each room has enough toothbrushes and napkin bibs. They make sure the tools they need are clean.

**Fun Fact:**
More than 166,000 dentists work in the United States.

7:30 in the morning

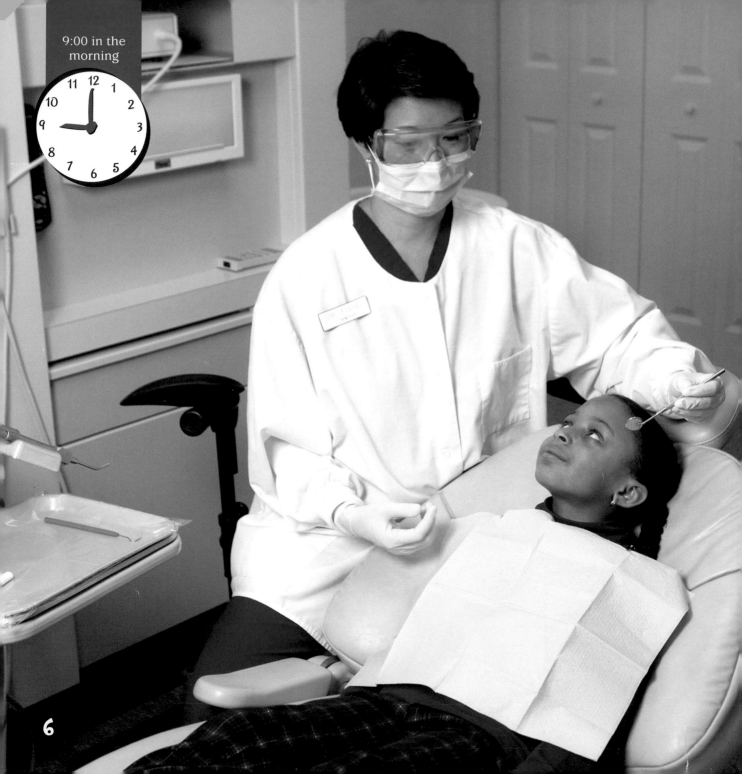

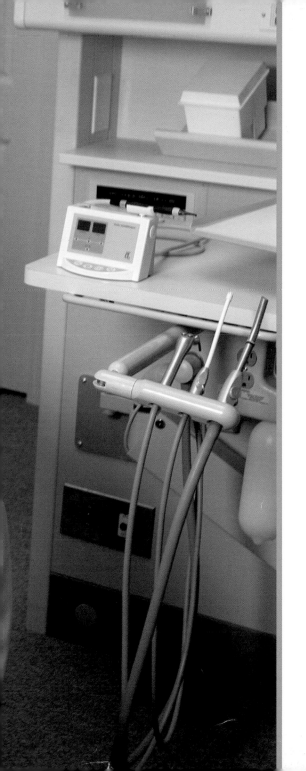

# What do dentists wear?

Dentists wear clothing that keeps them clean. Dr. Fong puts on gloves and a white coat. She wears a mask and glasses while looking in a patient's mouth. Wearing this clothing keeps Dr. Fong from spreading germs.

# Who helps dentists?

Dentists have many helpers. Dr. Fong's office manager greets patients. She also makes appointments and writes bills.

10:00 in the morning

Hygienists clean teeth. Assistants help dentists work with patients. Everyone works together to make the office run.

# What do dentists eat for lunch?

Dentists try to eat healthy foods like fruits and vegetables. Dentists know these foods help keep their teeth strong. Dr. Fong eats an apple with her lunch. She reads a book about new ways to fix teeth. After lunch, she brushes her teeth.

**Fun Fact:**

Sugary foods harm teeth. The sugar sticks to teeth and collects germs. The sugar and germs cause cavities.

# What happens at a checkup?

Checkups help dentists make sure a patient's mouth is healthy. Dr. Fong takes x-rays. She counts the patient's teeth and looks for tooth decay. She checks his gums for disease. Dr. Fong writes a report about each tooth. Sometimes she will put flouride on teeth to help prevent cavities.

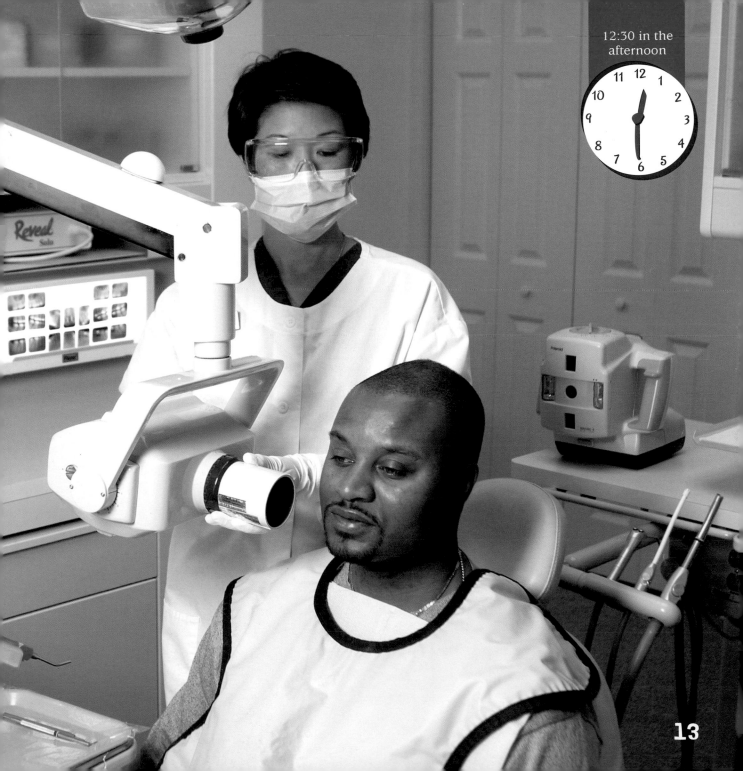

12:30 in the
afternoon

**13**

# What happens in a dentist's lab?

Labs are workrooms for dentists. Dentists can make models of teeth in their labs.

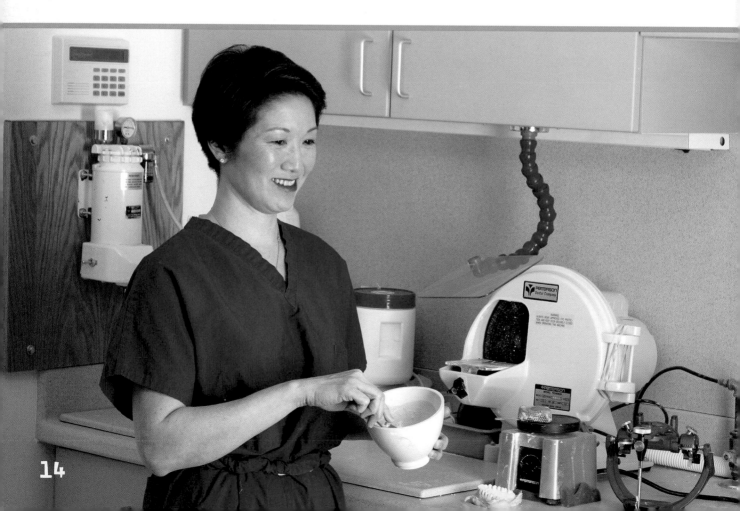

1:30 in the afternoon

Dr. Fong mixes plaster. She pours it into a mold shaped like her patient's teeth. The plaster hardens into a model. Dr. Fong uses the model to show the patient how she can repair his teeth.

# What tools do dentists use?

Dentists use many tools to keep teeth healthy. Dr. Fong uses a bright light and mirror to look in the patient's mouth. A small drill helps Dr. Fong repair a cavity. The assistant sucks out water and saliva with a vacuum straw. They repair the tooth together.

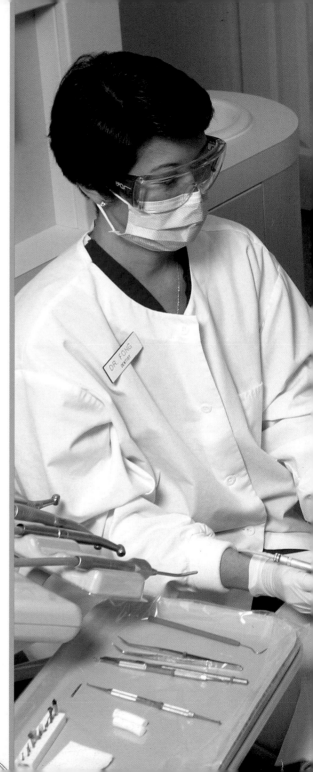

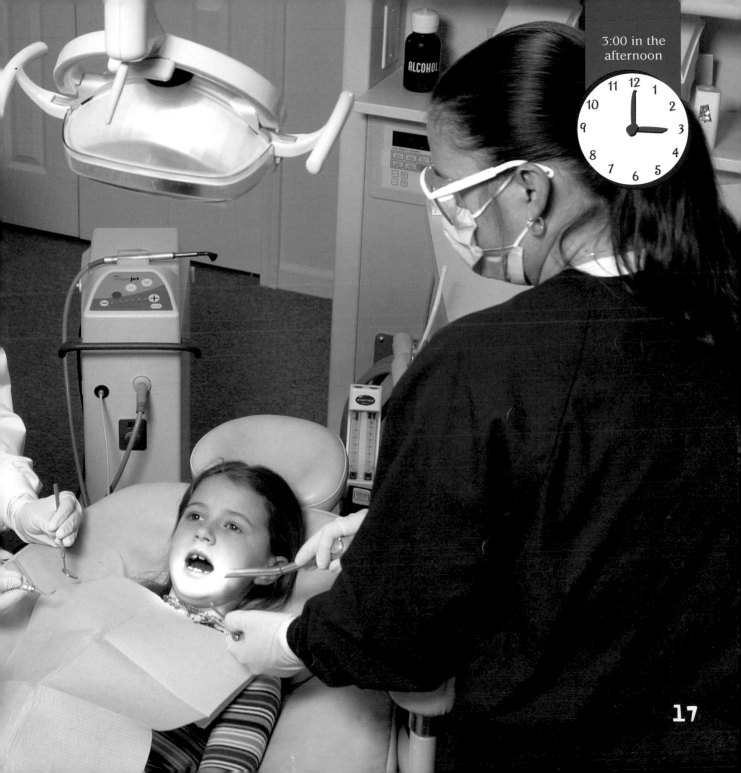

3:00 in the
afternoon

17

# Why do people need to visit the dentist?

Dentists help people take care of their mouths. Dr. Fong explains to a patient how sugar and germs damage teeth. She teaches him how to brush and use floss. Dr. Fong goes home knowing her patients have healthy teeth.

**Fun Fact:**

Most adults have between 28 and 32 teeth.

4:30 in the afternoon

## Amazing But True!

In 1498, a Chinese man made the first toothbrush. It had a bone handle and hog hair bristles. In 1938, an American company made a toothbrush with a plastic handle and nylon bristles.

**X-ray machine and x-rays**

**Powered handpieces** operate drills, polishers, and other tools for cleaning and repairing teeth.

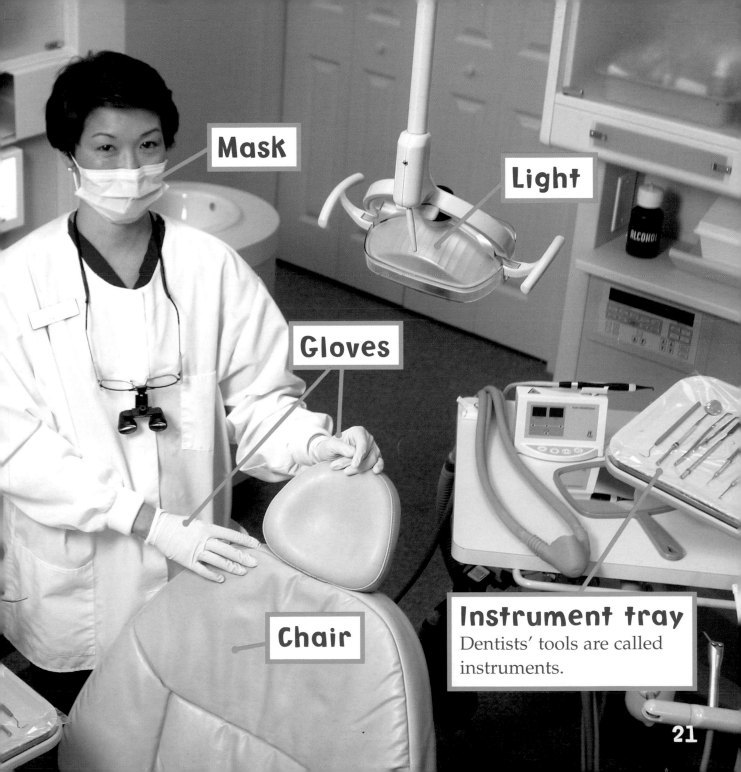

Mask

Light

Gloves

Instrument tray
Dentists' tools are called
instruments.

Chair

21

# Glossary

**appointment** (uh-POINT-muhnt)—an agreement to meet at a certain time

**cavity** (KAV-uh-tee)—a decayed or broken down part of a tooth

**clinic** (KLIN-ik)—a place where medical care is given; teeth are cared for at dental clinics.

**decay** (di-KAY)—rotting or breaking down

**disease** (duh-ZEEZ)—a sickness or illness

**germs** (JURMS)—small living things that cause disease

**hygienist** (hye-JEN-ist)—someone trained to know how to keep people clean and healthy; dental hygienists clean teeth.

**prevent** (pri-VENT)—to keep from happening

# Read More

**Bagley, Katie.** *Brush Well: a Look at Dental Care.* Your Health. Mankato, Minn.: Bridgestone Books, 2002.

**Gorman, Jacqueline Laks.** *Dentist.* People in My Community. Milwaukee: Weeky Reader Early Learning Library, 2002.

**Schaefer, Lola M.** *Dental Office.* Who Works Here? Chicago: Heinemann Library, 2000.

# Internet Sites

Do you want to find out more about dentists and teeth?
Let FactHound, our fact-finding hound dog,
do the research for you.

Here's how:
1) Visit *http://www.facthound.com*
2) Type in the **Book ID** number:
   **0736822828**
3) Click on **FETCH IT**.

FactHound will fetch Internet sites picked by our editors
just for you!

# Index

appointment, 8
assistant, 9, 16

bills, 8

cavity, 12, 16
checkup, 12

decay, 12
disease, 12
drill, 16

floss, 18
flouride, 12
fruits, 11

germs, 7, 18
glasses, 7
gloves, 7
gums, 12

hygienists, 9

labs, 14
light, 16

mask, 7
mirror, 16
model, 14–15
mold, 15

napkin bibs, 4

report, 12

saliva, 16
sugar, 18

toothbrushes, 4

vacuum straw, 16
vegetables, 11

white coat, 7

x-rays, 12